FLY GUY PRESENTS: DINOSAURS

Tedd Arnold

Scholastic Inc.

For my pal Wyatt—T.A.

ISBN 978-0-545-63159-4

24 23 22 21 20 19 18   16 17 18/0

Printed in the U.S.A.   40
First printing, January 2014
Designed by Rocco Melillo

A boy had a pet fly named Fly Guy.
Fly Guy could say the boy's name —

Buzz and Fly Guy were at the natural history museum (meu-ZEE-uhm).

"This museum has lots of cool stuff," said Buzz. "There are dinosaur bones in here."

Fly Guy was excited. They went inside
to learn about dinosaurs. . . .

PANGAEA

Dinosaurs walked the earth about 250
million years ago, during the Mesozoic
(mehz-uh-ZOH-ick) Era. Back then, all
the land on Earth was pushed together.
This landmass was called Pangaea
(pan-GEE-uh).

THE SEVEN CONTINENTS TODAY

Dinosaurs lived all across Pangaea.

Over millions of years, the land drifted apart to form seven continents.

TRICERATOPS

BRACHIOSAURUS

Humans did not live when dinosaurs were alive. But flies did!

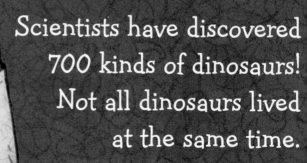

Scientists have discovered 700 kinds of dinosaurs! Not all dinosaurs lived at the same time.

For example, Tyrannosaurus rex
(tuh-ran-uh-SAWR-uhs reks) and
Stegosaurus (steh-guh-SAWR-uhs) never
met because they lived at different times.

Dinosaurs were reptiles. Reptiles are covered in scales.

Scales! →

Other reptiles include crocodiles, lizards, and turtles.

crocodile

lizard

turtle

Dinosaurs are also closely related to birds. That is because of how their leg bones join to their hips.

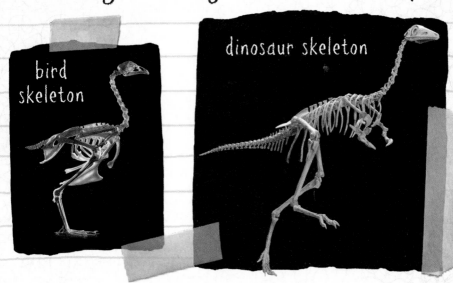

bird skeleton

dinosaur skeleton

All dinosaurs had scales, but some even had feathers, like birds.

feathered dinosaur

DINOSAUR EGG FOSSIL

HADROSAUR EGGS

DINOSAUR NEST

Baby dinosaurs hatched from eggs. Some eggs were as big as footballs. Others were small. Most dinosaur eggs were laid in nests on the ground.

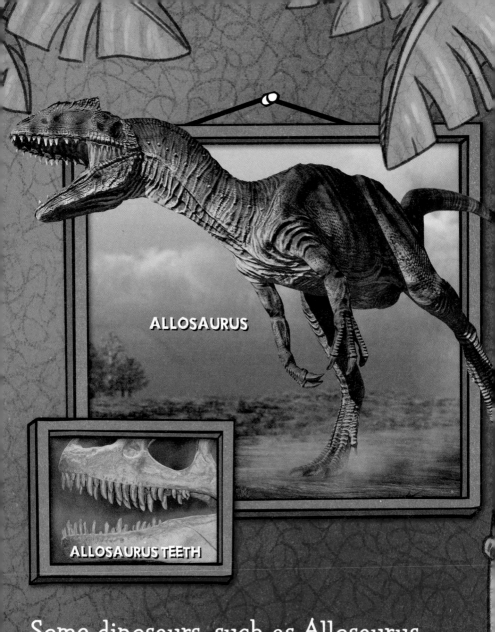

ALLOSAURUS

ALLOSAURUS TEETH

Some dinosaurs, such as Allosaurus (ah-loh-SAWR-uhs), ate other dinosaurs or animals. They were carnivores (CAHR-nih-vohrz). Carnivores had sharp teeth for hunting and chewing meat.

Other dinosaurs, like Iguanodon (ig-WAHN-uh-dohn), ate only plants. They were herbivores (HURB-ih-vohrz). Herbivores had flat teeth for chewing leaves.

VEGETARIANZZZ?

IGUANODONS

IGUANODON TEETH

MEAT TOOTH

VEGGIE TOOTH

Tyrannosaurus rex was a carnivore. T. rex had sharp teeth and claws. It could run fast, and had a good sense of smell.

T-rex

T-rex claws

T. rex was about forty feet long.
That's as long as a school bus!

T. rex was a great hunter.
That is why T. rex is called
"king of the dinosaurs."

Many dinosaurs, including T. rex, were predators (PREH-duh-turz). They hunted other dinosaurs or animals, called prey (PRAY). Dinosaurs had weapons to scare off predators or to hunt prey.

Many predators, like Velociraptor (veh-lohss-ih-RAHP-tur), had sharp teeth and claws.

VELOCIRAPTOR CLAW

Stegosaurus was an herbivore. It had a large, spiked tail to help keep predators away.

STEGOSAURUS TAIL

My body is my weapon!

Dinosaurs survived on Earth for a long time. So, were they supersmart?

They were good hunters and defenders. But most dinosaurs were no smarter than cats or dogs. Scientists believe that most dinosaurs had small brains. Stegosaurus had a brain the size of a walnut.

Many reptiles that lived in the Mesozoic Era were not dinosaurs. Dinosaurs lived only on land.

Pterosaurs (TEH-roh-sawrz) were flying reptiles. A Pterodactyl is a type of Pterosaur.

Pterodactyls

Pterodactyl landing

Plesiosaurs (PLEH-zee-oh-sawrz) lived in water during the time dinosaurs lived.

Plesiosaur

Pterosaurs and Plesiosaurs were not dinosaurs.

Dinosaurs ruled the planet for 165 million years. But about 65 million years ago, they all died out, or became extinct (eks-TINKT Scientists don't know why.

Some think a giant meteor hit Earth.
Others think an ash cloud from a volcano's
explosion blocked the sun, leaving the
dinosaurs with nothing to eat.

• VOLCANO ASH CLOUD •

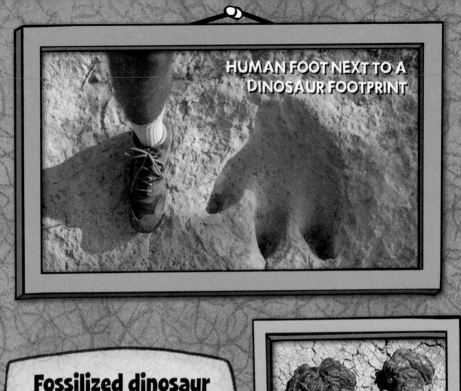

HUMAN FOOT NEXT TO A DINOSAUR FOOTPRINT

Fossilized dinosaur poop is called coprolite (CAH-pruh-lyt).

COPROLITE

Fossils are the remains of something that existed long ago.

PTERODACTYL FOSSIL

VELOCIRAPTOR SKULL

STEGOSAURUS SKELETON

They can be in rocks that formed over many years. Other fossils include dinosaur bones. Scientists have learned a lot about dinosaurs by uncovering fossils.

A paleontologist is a scientist who studies the history of life on Earth.

paleontologist in the lab

Paleontologists go on special trips called digs to look for dinosaur bones. When they find bones, they rebuild the skeleton.

Dig!

Each bone is dug up. Then it is cleaned.

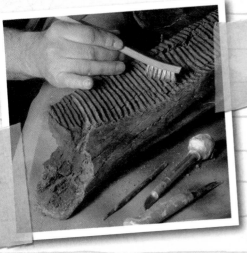

Next the scientists put the bones together like a very hard puzzle.

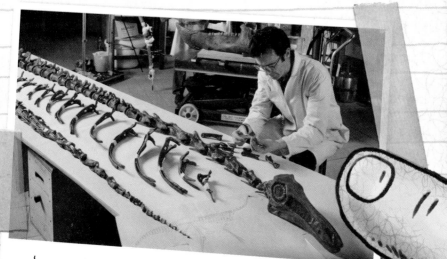

paleontologist building a dinosaur skeleton

Paleontologists sometimes make mistakes....
A paleontologist put the wrong skull on
an Apatosaurus (ah-pat-uh-SAWR-uhs)
skeleton. He thought it was a new kind
of dinosaur and called it Brontosaurus
(bron-tuh-SAWR-uhs) by mistake.

BISON

TRICERATOPS SKULL

In 1887, another paleontologist found a
skull in Wyoming. He thought it belonged
to an extinct bison. Later, he learned it
belonged to Triceratops (try-SEH-ruh-topz)!

Back at home, Buzz built a skeleton.

"Dinosaurs are awesome!" he said.
"I can't wait to go on another field trip!"